Come into the Garden

Di Sherlock

photographs by Anne Heslop

www.anneheslop.co.uk

cover and design by Andie Scott

www.andiescott.net

Foreword
by
Nell Dunn

This is an extraordinary poem telling the story of an ordinary family from Birmingham.

It is told by the daughter who chronicles the old age and death of her mother and father and the clearing and selling of the childhood home.

It is a love story of such beauty and depth it takes the breath away and teaches us everything there is to know about family life and family love.

N.D. December 2013

for Mum and Dad

Introduction

In 2004 I spent three months back in the family home convalescing from a severe eye haemorrhage, a lost job and a broken relationship.

I was the sick child and Mum and Dad took charge. As I watched their comings and goings I was moved to write. These poems form The Prologue.

Seven years go by. Then shortly after her 80th birthday my mother had a number of mini strokes, which brought on vascular dementia. At the same time my father was diagnosed with Non Hodgkin's Lymphoma. I was compelled to write again.

Despite doctors' predictions, Mum died after six months and Dad followed her eight months later. During this time I came home as much as I could to be with them. Mum's journey into dementia was something none of us were prepared for, least of all my valiant and despairing Dad. The roles of Child, Parent and Carer morphed constantly between us.

'Leaving the Garden' was written after I'd cleared the old house. It deals with memory and loss and my own transition to a new orphan state - that of the parentless adult child - which I believe is a neglected rite of passage no matter how old you are.

In the poems my mother is Florence, Maud and Betty. Florence is her Nurturing Self, Maud the Critic, Betty the Wife.

My father is Dennis.

My younger brother Mike is The Brother and The Son.

Dot is my mother's younger sister.

I am The Daughter.

The Lickeys are the Lickey Hills, South West of Birmingham, a bus ride from the family home, where we often went as kids, as did they.

Prologue

The Sick Child

She stands like a grey violet
Between her natural creation
Blighted in her bed
And her blooming artifice –
A little pot of apricot silk flowers
Dropped into the hub of the old coffee table
Draped with a cream crochet cloth
Like the dainty crinoline of a child princess
In the bay window.

Florence

Each morning
Florence opens the bedroom curtains
Like a daisy
To let the sun in,
Flashing her true smile behind false gnashers,
A perfect set
Exhibited with the grinning insistence
Of a death's head
All unbeknown to Florence,
But not to Maud
Of the sharp tongue and timely reminder
Of age's toll and the emptying of life's expectation
Never great to begin with.
The moon waxes and wanes over the dark conifer,
Lone nordic sentinel
Pointing to Florence's blue heaven
Where the birds sweeten her sleep
With their Evensong.

Heart of Amethyst

I knew I'd come to the right place
Despite all my fears to the contrary
When in the front room cabinet I espied
A heart of amethyst.
I washed the rock and explained to Florence
The healing properties of the glittering crystals
Which held her eye.
To which Maud replied,
If it fell on your toe
That would be something.

The Book

For the first time
Ever
Mum bought me a book,
Produced it with a bashful smile
Like a child exhibiting a school prize –
'Girl with a Pearl Earring'.
She wanted me to read it
Because it was good
Because she liked it
Because the painting by Vermeer on the cover
Had always reminded her of me as a girl
And it was time I shared her fiction.

Autumn Days

Dennis and Maud

Now the kids are gone
And the dog dead and buried,
He tends the garden he has taken over,
Raking and sweeping what was once Her terrain,
Silently observed
By Maud
Of the tight lip and the gimlet eye,
Protector of bulbs and merciless crusher
Of snails and blundering men.
He addresses the young shoots
As they were cubs,
Finally reaping
In this last repository of love.

Yesterday he mowed the lawn
And now the acer tree casts its shadow
Like crone's hair over the grass,
Clipped like a beard
For the dutiful planting
Of Maud's kiss.

He scoots like a schoolboy
On the supermarket trolley,
Dennis The Menace,
Watched by Maud of the irritable bowels,
Off to the recycling bins.
A little break for freedom,
A last jape at the Save A Can Centre
Before returning to Maud's absolute regime
Of elected victuals
All weighed and measured and salt-free
To keep the lid on the pressure cooker
Of their hearts.
Back in the garden
He hangs up the fat balls
To the epopeia of gluttonous tits and finches
Greedy for the feast.

Winter Comes

Falling

The long slanting rays of autumn have left
 And now it tends to winter.
Sunk in the gentle heart of Florence
Maud is leaving,
Leaving the garden to him.
One time half of a courting couple
She returns to those first times with gratitude.
He tends the garden now,
It's his job.
The abundance of apples that year
Has left the shelves
In kitchen, lounge and bedroom.
He's down to the last four,
The rest crunched away.

How did they go so fast?
What would she do without him,
Her brick?
Without her brick the house would fall down
As she does now without warning
Suddenly
The brain's hemispheres fizzing
Seizing her face in a mask of lost intention
As the darkness comes
The falling
She doesn't remember.

Dot

As she started to become
Invisible
The web she'd spun so tightly
Began to unravel.
First to blast through
Was her younger sister,
Voice gurgling down the phone
A lifetime's smoking
Given up now
Too late
No regrets.

A voice that dispelled the image
The other had made
Of an ogress,
Uncaring, uncharitable,
The voice was a voice
Of compassion and concern.
She'd worked in a Day Centre,
Knew what was what,
Knew what lay ahead
For a sister
A brother in law
Thinking to hide the vanishing
From the relatives.

Years knotted in
Separation
Stubbornness
Silence,
The aunt, the niece
Closer in age
Than the sisters,
Mother Daughter
Daughter Aunt,
Raising a wall
Now breached
In a strange new world of proximity.

I want you to tell Dennis
I care,
Said Auntie Dot.

Dot called,
I said,
She's going to call Mum on Sunday.

Not a good idea,
Said Dennis,
Be very careful.
She was angry when she saw your text
About Dot.

Don't call,
I said,
She'll bite your head off.

And Dot laughed
From the thick of her waterlogged chest
Like winter fields in Leicestershire.
Ok, she said,
But she called anyway.

Oh, said Florence,
Remembering nothing of all this,
It's lovely to hear from you!

Black and Chrome

This is the era of Black and Chrome

Pronounced Maud,

Perhaps alluding to the world of gadgets

Pictured in the magazine

Open in her lap,

Perhaps the world of the garden

As she gazed at bare soil,

Stripped back flower and bush

Tucked up tight for winter,

Dennis's handiwork

Not hers.

Her green fingers soothed the trembling stalks,

His hand the hand of the factory,

Years of beating and welding sheet metal

Into usefulness and a living

In the Midlands.

He knows what he's doing, she said,

Quieting the Daughter,

Do you want a green tea?

The Electric Steamer

She thought she'd do something to help
Health and Safety in the kitchen.
Visions of her mother buckling under the weight
Of the ancient pressure cooker,
Fiddling with the knob that took too long
To pop up,
Fingers tapping the handles,
Trying to crack the code,
Fingers that are also learning
To let go.
Unbearable.
And so she ordered an electric steamer.
Don't tell her, said Dennis,
We'll wait for it to arrive,
Deal with it then.

But she couldn't stop herself,
Let slip that evening in the kitchen
As she kept a wary eye on Florence
Around the pressure cooker.
You haven't gone and got one have you?
Flashed Maud
In a rare comeback,
Wielding the pressure cooker
Like the sword of the Nibelungs.

They're not delivering it here are they?
Yes, she said with a spry smile,
Intending to communicate ease and effortlessness,
The lightest of culinary magic
As the broccoli and potatoes steamed to a mulch
In the belly of the pressure cooker.

Days later, standing in her own kitchen
A world away,
A sudden text from Dennis:
The cooker has landed
And is being viewed with suspicion.
Days pass.
No mention of the steamer.
Then a text from Florence
Finally
Blown across the airwaves
Like a kiss:
Just going to try it out love,
Will let you know how we get on.

But how duplicitous
A kiss!
When next she visited
The steamer had become an excuse
To give up cooking altogether.
Now Dennis fiddles with the timer,
Confounding time
As he masters his new tool.

End of the Old

She turns the pages of the newspaper
Like an oracle,
Seeing only with the inner eye,
Gazing at the incomprehensible world
She is turning her back on
Defiant.

Husband and Daughter,
Staring stubbornly at the telly,
Try not to let the irritable rustling
Interfere with the international banking conspiracy
That holds their minds temporarily
In suspension.

The world turns around the armchair now,
Throne, seat, dominion,
Things dropped plummet
Into a sea of magazines,
The last wires
Of a fictional network she holds onto
To pass the time.

Outside the window

Whose eye opens and closes

With the parting of the curtains,

The snow thaws

Meets the dismal fog.

The bright icicle that hung

From the clothes line for days,

An architectural wonder,

Is melting into air

Heavy with moisture

And the end of things.

Flower Days

Do you think I'm a burden?
Asked Florence,
As they made their way to the library,
Holding the Daughter's arm, supported
By the American belt
Dennis got from the chiropractor.
Dennis' new regime
Saw an end to the dominion of The Armchair.
A small triumph.

You're my Mum,
Is all the Daughter can say,
Heart struck.
Then quickly, lest emotion flood
The fragile intimacy, adds
Who put that idea in your head?
I sometimes think, said Florence,
Treading cautiously,
That Dennis thinks I'm a burden.

Later that evening
Florence turns to her,
Do you know what I'd like?
She says sadly,
I'd like some perfume.

Back home
Florence's words float into the night,
A sorrowful cloud
Of English lavender, rose, lily of the valley,
An apology for old age
And wishfulness,
Words that remind the Daughter
Of the absence of perfume in her own life,
Of lost intimacy
And the long years of self help
Within monastic walls.

Oh
The flower days
That they might come again!

I must get her some perfume
She determined,
Trying to exorcise Florence from her thoughts,
And get myself a make over
Before it's too late.

Dennis

I'd like a week's holiday,
Said Florence,
Looking out at the first signs of Spring in the garden,
The budding bush she'd once known the name of,
Had told the Daughter who never remembered
More than once.

Clematis?

But it's Dennis who needs the holiday.
Combusting at an ill timed remark
By the Daughter,
Misconstruing a casual comment,

Tipping all thought
Of further discussion
Into the fiery furnace.

The Daughter sees his own father
Emerging with such clarity now
As he raises his head,
Blue boned, blue veined,
So very tired, so very stubborn,
One last flex of inflexible
Muscle knuckled mind.

His poor tired face worn thin
With Florence's nonsense.
Her wandering off in Sainsbury's
Away from where he'd stationed her
By her comics, as he calls them -
Woman's Weekly, Woman's Own, Take a Break -
The shedding of clothes on the floor
Till put by him in the wash basket.

One machine he still resists
Insisting it is her domain –
The washing machine –
Despite the mystified staring at the wash cycles,
The confusion round the on / off button
And the wrenching of the clenched door
Before time.
But something she should still be in charge of.

Though he has learned to toss mushrooms in butter
For mushrooms on toast.
It is only a matter of time
Before the washing machine too
Falls
Into the hands of the maladroit god
Of iron and steel.
Only a matter of time
Before the last veil of Vesta
Descends
To lie abandoned,
Like Florence's white hankie
Under the radiator.

In the Carvery

Out for lunch at the Carvery
Dennis unwittingly makes Florence cry.
He never says nice things about me,
She says, tears welling
In luminous eyes
Still beautiful
Pools of green grey
In the dear faded face.
The Daughter hears the words
She once uttered herself,
Another life
Still quick wound of memory,

Reaches over to stroke
The crumpled hand.

Dennis, trouncing all sentiment,
Especially tears,
Slices on.
You're still here aren't you?
He says,
Downing the last of his pint.
The Daughter bites her tongue,
Remembering the need for a kind word
As a drink in the desert she thirsted for herself
And never got in those moments,
Takes the cut deeper than Florence.

Later
She texts the Brother,
Mainly silent in London
Or elsewhere in Business Class.
Oh God, he says,
I didn't realise it was so bad.
But it is.
And it isn't.

Years of mutual bullying and manipulation
Have settled like dust between them
Now rising and falling again
In a perfect storm
Of misplaced credit cards
Lost keys
And false teeth in remarkable places,
Of lost companionship
Servitude
And the dread of being the one
Left.

Spring Returns

Smile

When she entered the house
For the first time
Since Death had come
It felt
Like the space left
After a bird has flown
Like the involuntary gasp
That follows a smile of recognition.

Rainbow

In the yard
Where her Mother used to sit,
Fragile now,
Seat carefully positioned
So the sun's rays struck her
Like first light at the solstice,
The Daughter sees
The azalea bush
They'd admired only two weeks before
Quite blown away.

Only half of it flowered this year,
The Mother had said,
Gazing with the Daughter on the effusion
Of apricot, pink and tangerine
In quiet rapture.

The Daughter stands in the yard,
The empty seat still in position,
The flowers strewn,
And sees a sympathetic ghost
Gone early
But in time
For her Mother to enjoy a last flowering
Of Spring on Earth.

Later,
As she walked to the station
Past the church
Where soon the little service would happen
She'd yet to sort,

Evening now,
Stormy spring clouds,
She wept
Celebrating her Mother's final freedom
From pain.

From back pain, hip pain
And the darker pain
Of knowing your mind is slipping away
Taking with it your last grace and dignity,
As if a sudden interloper
Had made off with your partner at the dance,
Leaving you foolish and humiliated and alone.

And as she praised her mother's willful spirit
The sun shot out of the darkness
And there appeared
Half a rainbow,
One half hidden,
A mystery,
The other shining clear
With the radiance of a smile.

Marigolds

In the florists next to the undertakers
The Daughter searches for clues.
What flowers what colours what
For that last bouquet?
Gets it wrong,
The pinks and whites and apricots are for a bride,
Oh God,
Remembers the mother's dream of marigolds,
Gets it right.
The tangerine and yellow of the gerbera
Dance for joy
Among the white and peach of the roses.
Our Betty's colours,
Says Dot affirmatively,
As demurely slipping from the limo
The coffin makes its entrance.

Now Dennis fills the lonely patio
With marigolds.
He wishes she could see them,
His beloved Betty,
Gather them in her green and mortal eye
Now closed to him.

In their brightness
They take him back,
To the dance hall
Where first she caught him
Off guard,
The Wife to be.

Blessing

Every evening after the funeral
The Daughter went into the garden
And gazed at the sky.
Two long vapour trails of cloud
Stretched like wings
Rose feather light
Against the night
Impending.

A lone gull
Wheeled around the houses
Over and over
Like a cradling,
Two swallows faded
High
In an invisible kiss.

Mum's Birmingham

When she was a girl
All full of oak and chestnut
And moon of blue willow in the morning,
She rode her bike through laughing cow parsley,
Clover and speedwell,
Freewheeling through the birdsong
Heart free,
Leaving an invisible trace
That now the Daughter tracks.

Bees in the daisies blessing her notebook,
The Daughter follows the Mother's trail
To find the girl in the vanishing.
Coming to understand why
Her Mother loved this place
She'd never seen in June.
It was always the edge of autumn

Speaking winter in eye and bone
When she visited.
But now blown roses,
Tree speak, bird speak,
Grass and flower speak,
Ancient dream in the suburbs.

She sits and writes.
A huffing Labrador, plump on lead life,
'NO BALL GAMES'
Gives a tug of recognition
Of Wild Time
When dogs ran free over the Lickeys
And dreamed
The hunter's dream,
The shepherd's dream,
The dream of limb and loin in the dawning.

Oh to find that laughing girl
Before the loss of elm and air.
The Grandmother's house
Once so enormous
Shrunken
In the cold light of adult eye.
Hard to imagine
All that life
In a humble council house,
The Brother had said.

Summer

Early July Morning in Birmingham

The Mother looks over from The Other Side
And sees the solitary Daughter
Amongst the nettles
Thinking of her
As she folds choice leaves in kitchen roll
For later decoction.
Each sees the other young again,
The Daughter the Mother in her courting days
Laughing to camera,
Boldly shy in her headscarf and heels,
A touch of the Rita Hayworths
In the mane of auburn hair framed in the wind.
The Mother the Daughter as a child
Seeking out impossible places,
Enthroned in an ants' nest,
Shaking bees from flowers,
Never stung
Til the soft halo of infancy was no more.
And so each touches the other
Crossing worlds
In an unseen act of love.

Early July Morning on Holy Island

The solitary Daughter walks the dunes
Sings to the sea
The sound is always
Ma Ma.

The solitary Daughter wades in the icy water,
Picks her way across the sharpness of shell.
She hears the infant moan of the wind,
The siren song of the seals,
Walks the flat grey of sea and sky,
Reflected in the luminous sand
Beneath her feet a sudden glimpse
Of a nether sun.

She thinks of her mother in her last days,
Head upturned like a sunflower,
Her smile at the touch of heat and light,
Beatific.

Later,
She finds a dead seal on the rocks,
A young one,
She thinks perhaps the siren song
Was after all a litany,
The plainsong wail of maternal love.

The Stone

The Father and the Daughter
Survey the Mother's 'plot',
The little mound of naked earth
Unmarked
Where the ashes are buried.
He'd got her in
In the nick of time.
Only two plots left
In that wild corner.

Lying in wait outside the church
He'd never gone to,
He'd ambushed the Vicar after Sunday Service,
Was received with loving kindness,
Blessed
And the deal with God was made.

The Daughter holds a floral tribute from the garden,
Seven yellow, black-eyed daisies
From Dennis' proud team
And some lavender she'd swiped on the way.
She places it gently on the plot
Traced lovingly by Dennis' finger in the clay.

He eyes the desolation of dead flowers
On the surrounding stones,
Her neighbours,
As the Daughter hunts around for something
To secure the daisies.

She places a stone
Fished from the compost heap.
He watches with tearful eye,
Wanting a proper stone
To cover that place,
Betty's place,
And a lighter grey than church regulation *Rustenberg.*

The Daughter fears her Father's ruminations
On the graves which seem forgotten,
Unkempt,
Will bring him to pronounce on
The extinction of his own line,
As neither she nor the Brother have offspring
And when his time comes to join the Loved One
Down there,
Who to bring fresh flowers on a Sunday
To Birmingham?
But he says nothing.

They stand in silence

For a while

Looking at the bright spill of the daisies,

Then with one breath

They turn and head back.

It Ends and It Begins

September Before The Fall

The Daughter
Sits in the Mother's chair,
Sees the new moon
Ghosting
In the bright morning.

She surveys the garden
Turning to autumn,
Wonders what will become of it
When the Father goes.

How to turn away from all that love
Fed and watered and weeded,
The soft perishable of spent fruit
Entrusted.
How to leave all this behind,
Sell up and go,
Embrace the world again.
How do they do it those other people?
Grief bubbles up.
She goes back into the house,
Thankful the Father still bumbles
Amongst the impossible roses.
She packs her case.

Back home,
She whirrs round the kitchen
Like a ballerina in a musical box,
Trying to make a whole of herself,
Allocating bits to fridge and cooker and bin,
One last tidy revolution
Before the call she does not want to make.

The Father answers, pinched with pain,
Something dark trapped in his leg,
Something that will mean the fall
Down the hall stairs
Along hospital corridors
Into the wrong wards,

In and out of Centres and Units
Until finally he comes to a rest of sorts
In the kindly lap of the Nursing Home.   .
The Stone is on its way,
He says,
Docking in a week.

She slumps on the sofa,
Looks at the smiling photo of the Mother
In her little world of beige.
Great waves of grief roll over and under -
Packed lunches of cheese and marmite,
Sainsbury's vouchers saved for her,
Little gifts of money for a day by the sea.

The Brother is sympathetic.
Her text reminds him of his own loss,
The Father's cancer usurping the grief
That was the Mother's.
We both are due a holiday, he says,
But he cancels his.

The Daffodils

When the Daughter returned
From the meeting with the Registrar,
Stone in heart, unbelieving –
The man did not know her father,
Hell bent on putting
The hateful year behind him –
When she returned,
Smile mask in position,
He fixed her with his one good eye and said,
I thought I'd at least make it to the Spring!
Mortified, she lied,
No one said you wouldn't, Dad.
But the Registrar had said
Dead by Christmas.

In a corner of the front garden,
Always his domain,
The Mother had no interest in that lawless patch
Flanking car and step,
There now began a pushing and swelling
Beneath the frozen earth,
Driving juice green flow against the clock.

And lo!

Three daffodils burst through the January snow,

Loyal against all odds,

Sounding the trumpet for Dennis

Who put the old behind him

Against all odds

In a miracle of Spring.

FROM CADBURY'S FACTORY IN A GARDEN BOURNVILLE.

Pain

In the long night of the virus
She was tormented by images
Of her father's pain,
Saw him dangling in the hoist
Like an insect
Broken
A sight he forbade her to witness.

But somehow she'd got trapped in the room
By the well intentioned clumsy new carer
Who did it wrong.
Dropped him.
A supernova of pain
Had him crying like a beaten dog.
Oh these things she wished she had not seen.

Coughing and sweating
In the hour before sudden dawn,
His pain, her pain,
Moments in colossal time.
Oh Dad.

The Dreaming Hand

Towards the end
The hands that hammered sheet metal,
Birmingham hands,
Wove the air with the delicacy
Of Japanese fans,
The hopeless fragility of moths
Fluttering round the beaker
He could not get a grip of.
The humiliation of juice spilled,
Tea abandoned
In the comfy Nursing Home.

The Daughter gazed at the long elegant fingers
With the thick gold band
That was his father's father's
With fascination.
In his sleep he moves the useless right hand
Like a blind piano player.
She had never really noticed his hands before,
Never really looked,
Though felt their fury as an adolescent,
Assumed them rough and hard,
Industrial.

But now she sees the fingers of the soul

That had emerged to paint in oils

Once his working days were done,

Tracing familiar landscapes

And apocalyptic skies in winter,

(Though he did not care for William Blake)

Hidden for so long

They are apparent now

In the symphony of the dreaming hand.

Rough Passage

His bed a boat of pain.
The new moon,
Horned boat of Osiris,
Sails on a starry sky.

How much longer?
He asks,
As the tea trolley rattles in the corridor
Of the comfy Nursing Home.

The Daughter, not wanting to be fatuous,
Says nothing,
Then makes a fatuous reply,
Til tea, Dad? Half an hour.

She watches the dry lips murmur the mantra
Half an hour
Aghast,
Resolves to be real next time.

Then suddenly he shouts,
What am I supposed to do now?
Another unanswerable question.
She does her best.

You don't have to do anything, Dad,
She says,
Just hold steady.
He grips the guard rail as the bed
Tosses blindly in the storm.

The Daughter cedes to the Brother,
He keeps the last watch.
Ripped on a surf of unknowing
The Father rocks into fathomless blue.

Leaving the Garden

Memories

In the long summer of
The Cancer
He would shake them from their bed,
Daughter and Son,
Like bugs from a bloom
And get them into the garden.
7am
Sun high already
Work to be done
So much work to be done.
Cup of tea, then cap on naked skull
And into the garden
With a vengeance.
Flying on post chemo steroid high
He commanded the slackers.

Three months after the funeral
The Daughter remembers all this,
Suddenly gets the loss of him.
Sees him
Sitting on the back step
Mug of tea in hand,
Surveying the fruits of mutual hard labour
With grudging eye.

Never a thought of Death.
Or so it seemed
To her.

But what drove him to that last heroic stand
Against dereliction
Of garden and gland
Knew
Mower and Shears were temporal.

Eastbourne

For a year after her Mother's death
She could not come to this place,
Eastbourne,
Ticket gifted by her Mother
They'd share the day by text.
Now she returns.

Away from the boom of the shore
The white convolvulus sounds
A silent trumpet
As she heads for The Downs.
The Father had said
No man should leave this earth
Without some mark, some remembrance
That he had once been.
In The Birmingham Post she'd put an obituary
Fierce and fitting
Approved by the Brother.

But the Mother had been happy to melt away
Without a fuss.
Where are you Mum?
In the purple wildflowers whose names you knew?
In the wake of the blue butterflies?
In the familiar wind that points tree and bush?
Threading an invisible line of memory
You quiet the clamour of the world.

Exchange

The Daughter races for the bus
Stops herself
Goes and sits in the Cathedral.
These are, after all, the last days.
Behind her Burne-Jones' angels
Spread Armageddon crimson wings
Decorous but brutal.
She thinks of the Brother
Business as usual
While she is left
To organise the final clearance
Of furniture and shed.
Only two days between exchange and completion
Thanks to the bully at the bottom of the chain.
So unfair
So selfishly male
Enough of that.

Distilled in the bus ride home
Her own story:
She passes the school that made her,
The hospital where she trailed the Father all summer
To the chemo bag,

Cursing as he barked at her to keep up
Though she did not know the way
In that featureless landscape,
Past the posh suburb that wasn't so posh
When her mother went to school there,
Rehoused from the Bell Barn Road slum
She shone and had her light put out
By poverty and domestic servitude,
But passed it to the Daughter in the cellular dark,
Past the Uni where she taught one semester a year
To be with them
And was surprised by a love of teaching,
And finally to the house,
To tip the last items of memory
And hand them, unrecyclable, to Tony and Sons,
Who bickered in the shed but did a good job.

When she'd arrived at the station
She had not really thought about it,
She had a job to do.
After weeks of deadlock down the chain
They had finally exchanged.
But when she hit the street she suddenly felt
All hollowed out
As if she'd had a hysterectomy of the self.

But it was just the Child
Set free for the last time
Clutching at the phantom umbilical chord
Like a demented amputee.
She wondered if the bully at the bottom of the chain
Was not after all the angel with the fiery sword
Sent by Mum and Dad.
The date of completion is her birthday.

Completion

I lay out the body of the naked house
Like a new born babe or corpse
The empty rooms suspend
Expectant
And we are gone already
The Sherlocks.